REGGIE MILLER

From Downtown

by

Joe Frisaro

SPORTS PUBLISHING INC.
www.SportsPublishingInc.com

©2000 Sports Publishing Inc.
All rights reserved.

Series editor: Rob Rains
Production manager: Susan M. McKinney
Production coordinator: Erin J. Sands
Cover design: Scot Muncaster/Todd Lauer
Photo editor: Terrence C. Miltner
Photos: AP/Wide World Photos, Brian Spurlock, UCLA

ISBN: 1-58261-180-7
Library of Congress Catalog Card Number: 99-68624

SPORTS PUBLISHING INC.
www.SportsPublishingInc.com

Printed in the United States.

Contents

Reggie Miller is a player who thrives on the pressure of a big game. (AP/Wide World Photos)

CHAPTER ONE

Lights Go Out on Broadway

Stars covet the big stage, at least the real ones do. They bask in the spotlight, radiate in the attention and deliver in the clutch.

When it comes to pure theatrics in the National Basketball Association no place touches Madison Square Garden in New York City. And few athletes have risen to the occasion in this historic building more often than Reggie Miller of the Indiana Pacers.

Under the hot lights in New York, Reggie has turned in some of the most electrifying individual moments ever in NBA playoff history.

Reggie Miller is the player New York fans love to hate. Jeers of "Reggie! Reggie!" ring from the rafters whenever the Knicks square off against the Pacers.

It doesn't bother Reggie in the least because he is comfortable playing the role of villain. In fact, he thrives on it. He enjoys playing games on the road for that purpose: To hear the crowds cheering against him. On the baseball court, few things get his motor running like boo-birds.

"I've been with players who have taken advantage of their superstardom," said Pacers backup center Sam Perkins, a seasoned veteran who was a college teammate of Michael Jordan at North Carolina.

"I think Reggie is just a level-headed, cool guy. But his temperament on the court, his demeanor is almost like he is out there to punish whoever tries to guard him. That's the attitude he takes. He works hard—he's there every day.

"I've been around a lot of superstars who had a lot of talent, but they don't have anything to show for it. All they wanted to do was make the headlines. Reggie is one of the leaders on this team. He's hungry out there. He wants to win so bad, and that's what you really love about him. I give him straight A's all across."

New Yorkers relish in the chance to rile up Reggie. It's all in good fun, and generates excitement.

In this hostile environment, Reggie has pulled off some legendary accomplishments. There was Game 5 in the 1994 playoffs when he pumped in 25 points in the fourth quarter alone (including a

Reggie makes his way off the court after defeating the Knicks in the 1998 NBA playoffs. (AP/Wide World Photos)

playoff record five 3-pointers in the period). Then, in the 1995 playoffs, Reggie worked a miracle—scoring eight points in an 8.9 second span that rallied the Pacers from six down to a 107-105 victory in the final 16 seconds.

As if these feats aren't enough, more Reggie magic took place at the Garden in the 1998 playoffs. Again, with the Pacers on the brink of defeat, Reggie buried a 3-point shot in the waning moments that enabled Indiana to eliminate New York in five games.

Reggie saves his best moments for New York's big stage.

When facing the Knicks in New York, Reggie becomes more than just a basketball player. He's a performer. And his antics make headlines. He's had a long-running feud with film maker Spike Lee, the most ardent of all Knicks' fans.

That's why Reggie Miller wanted yet another crack at the Knicks in the 1999 Eastern Conference Finals. The competitor in him said: "Bring it on."

"You're probably playing in the greatest basketball arena in the world," Reggie says. "So if you can't get pumped up at Madison Square Garden . . ."

So the stage was set. Reggie and the Pacers were in the Eastern Conference Finals for the second straight year. Standing in their way were the always aggressive Knicks.

Another battle was about to unfold.

"They're made up of a bunch of guys that hold, hit—there's a lot of thugging going on." Reggie said before the series started. "And we like that.

"For so long, everyone has kind of constituted New York as the bullies on the block. They are in the media capital of the world. They get all the attention. Everyone complains that we are the kids from Indiana. We are never on TV. It's like I was going to the big city for the first time. I like my chances—we are a good team."

Reggie was ready to battle. The Pacers played up their small-market status, while the New York media dubbed the series: "Knicks vs. Hicks."

But this time around, Reggie lost his magical touch—and the heavily-favored Pacers dropped the series in six games.

Reggie failed to find the scoring groove he had in the first two rounds of the playoffs. He averaged 26.3 and 21.8 points per game, respectively, in sweeps over Milwaukee and Philadelphia.

Determined not to let Reggie beat them again, New York used the philosophy—"let the rest of the Pacers beat us." Reggie managed just 16.2 points a game over the series.

Reggie and the Pacers came up short against Latrell Sprewell and the New York Knicks in the 1999 Eastern Conference Finals. (AP/ Wide World Photos)

The most gut-wrenching game, for him, was the last one. Fittingly, Reggie was at Madison Square Garden. But Reggie's deadly shot was off.

The Knicks prevailed 90-82 on a night nothing fell for Reggie Miller. The Pacers primary scoring weapon, and designated New York killer, pumped in just eight points on three of 18 shooting. He didn't score in the fourth quarter.

New York's Allan Houston, assigned to cover Reggie, finished with 32 points. In a twist of fate, the series ultimately was decided by a shooting guard not named Reggie Miller.

"Horrendous. Horrendous. A lot of open looks," Reggie told reporters at the news conference. "They (Pacers) were looking to ride my back this round, and I didn't do it for the them."

Reggie took the series loss hard.

Indiana indeed underachieved in the lockout-shortened 1999 season. Once Michael Jordan retired, the Pacers were anointed favorites to win the Eastern Conference championship, if not the NBA title.

As a leader on a veteran team, Reggie Miller expected nothing less. So he shouldered the blame when the season was lost. In the process, he showed a side of himself that contrasts the "bad boy" public image he purposely displays.

As a player, Reggie is a fierce competitor. As a team player, he demonstrates class and character.

"I have to take responsibility because I definitely feel like I let our franchise down—really our state," Reggie said. "For me to come up short in such a critical point and a critical time, it's very difficult."

You measure true leadership by how one reacts in the face of adversity. In this regard, Reggie scored points with his postgame comments, even if he had a tough night putting the ball in the basket.

Reggie is fully aware of his standing with the Pacers, his teammates, the organization and the state of Indiana, which calls itself the "heart of basketball country."

It is so easy to say the right things after a victory. Rising up and accepting accountability on the night of a disappointing loss is something else.

Reggie not only publicly accepted responsibility, he later gave a heartfelt congratulations to Allan Houston in the hallway.

As Houston was walking to the interview room to address reporters, Reggie stopped him.

"You can do it," Reggie said, implying the Knicks could win the overall title against the San Antonio Spurs.

Houston shrugged.

But Reggie drove the point home by repeating his words, with more force: "No, you guys can re-

Everyone thought 1999 would be the Pacers' year. But it wasn't meant to be. (AP/Wide World Photos)

ally do it," An appreciative Allan Houston nodded.

For the Knicks, it wasn't meant to be. The Spurs were too much for New York, taking the NBA championship in five games.

A title wasn't meant to be for Reggie Miller and the Indiana Pacers either in 1999. For the franchise, another opportunity to wear a championship ring was lost. But falling short didn't come from a lack of preparation.

Reggie and his teammates put in the work hours. They just didn't get the results they had hoped for.

Reggie made sure the Pacers would be ready for the 1999 season by leading workouts during the lockout. (AP/Wide World Photos)

CHAPTER TWO

Co-head Coach Reggie

From the outset, 1999 was not your typical NBA season. A lingering labor dispute caused the owners to lock out the players, resulting in the league shutting down for six months. The sport took another hit when the great Michael Jordan announced his retirement after leading the Chicago Bulls to six championships in eight years.

For months people wondered if indeed there would be a season. Training camp was lost. No formal practices were scheduled. Many players didn't put in the work necessary to be ready when the lockout ended.

Not the Pacers. Thanks to the efforts of Reggie Miller and guard Mark Jackson, the players prepared on their own—not knowing if their time would be rewarded.

"We've known each other for a long time now." Mark Jackson says. "I consider him Batman and me Robin. We are two guys who are a lot alike. We love to argue. We love to disagree. We love sports. We really get along well. It's just a great relationship that I'm really proud of, because he is a heck of a guy."

Such a bond made the Pacers the envy of the league, earning respect from the media nationally, while sending a message to the people in Indiana that their team was willing to work, despite the adversity.

During the lockout, league rules prohibited players from training at team facilities. Reggie and Mark made other arrangements. They gathered at the home of Indianapolis businessman Stephen Hilbert, a local billionaire and long-time courtside season-ticket holder.

Hilbert is Chairman and CEO of Conseco, a insurance/financial services company that has the naming rights to the Conseco Fieldhouse, the new home of the Pacers.

Hilbert's home includes a sizable basketball court.

The players used Hilbert's place until they found an alternative site, an Indianapolis health club, which accommodated the Pacers by placing a wooden basketball court over some indoor tennis courts.

After losing to the Chicago Bulls and Michael Jordan in the 1998 Eastern Conference Finals, Reggie wanted to be sure the Pacers were ready for the 1999 season. (Brian Spurlock)

Reggie and Mark assumed the roles of co-head coaches. They made the calls to their teammates, and conducted drills, much like the team would do if there was no lockout.

Assembling their teammates really was not much of a problem. Many are veterans who were hungry to reach the NBA Finals, especially after they lost a seven-game series to the Chicago Bulls in the 1998 Eastern Conference Finals.

Indiana dropped the decisive Game 7 on the road, after leading late in the game. The Pacers viewed their off-season dedication as a chance to gain homecourt advantage in the playoffs.

"When we got on the phone and told the guys, they remembered the taste that we had in our mouths when we lost to Chicago, and how much of a difference it would have been if we had home court advantage," Mark said. "That's one game, that's two games, that's a loose ball. And if you put the time in, those things are going to happen."

The Pacers have never reached the NBA Finals. The team was willing to put in the hours to make 1999 their year.

Many of the experts thought so, picking Indiana to fill the championship seat Chicago held for so long.

Such championship talk did not set well with Reggie Miller, who downplayed the expectations. Hard work alone is not enough.

"The title will happen if we take care of business," Reggie said after a preseason workout before the lockout settled. "I can't say we are going to win the title this year. I don't like it when guys do that. Go out and play and perform and let the chips fall where they may."

The Pacers are a veteran team that had reached

the Eastern Conference Finals three times in their history—1993-94, 1994-95 and 1997-98. In all three cases, they lost game seven on the road. At home, the outcomes might have been different.

Indiana coveted home court, because they were so successful there. In 1998, for example, they were a perfect 8-0 at Market Square Arena.

"In all three (Conference) finals we had a chance to move on to the NBA Finals, but we lost on the road," Reggie said. "Yes, home court is important. But I'd like to think we are still a crafty, veteran team. If we had to go to somebody's house to win a game, I think we could. But it's always good to have the comforts of home."

The Pacers felt they gave the Bulls their biggest scare in 1998. Indiana took Chicago to the brink of elimination in Game 7 at the United Center before losing in the closing minutes.

Reggie is always ready to work hard, on or off the court.
(AP/Wide World Photos)

"We feel we took a lot out of them," Reggie said. "Of course, our guys were disappointed. So now you look at the little things. Could that series have been conditioning?"

If so, the Pacers were prepared to push harder, if that is what it took to gain an extra edge. At age 33, Reggie was entering his 11th NBA season. Opportunities to win it all were winding down.

Conditioning became a primary focus at the workouts led by co-coaches Reggie and Mark.

The Pacers pride themselves as an unselfish team, comprised of humbled stars that get along.

"Getting the guys out here wasn't the hard part," Reggie said. "Finding a place to get started was."

Substituting for the Pacers real coach, legendary Larry Bird, Reggie and Mark emphasized drills and conditioning as much as scrimmages.

"We didn't want to kill guys," Reggie said. "But on the other hand, we wanted to get something out of it. If guys were going to sacrifice and come out here, we wanted to make it productive. We didn't just want to scrimmage. That's the easy way out. I've always felt you don't get everything done during scrimmages because sometimes your play is called and other times it's not. So we did a lot of drills, a lot of conditioning."

Reggie has never ducked hard work. He is among the league's most active players on the court. He is constantly moving, attempting to get free for a long-range jumper. And as the Pacers primary scoring threat, Reggie often works against the opposition's top defender.

Being in tip-top shape is crucial. It comes with the territory of being a professional athlete.

Reggie, especially, does not take conditioning for granted, because at one point in his life, doctors doubted if he would ever take that major step into athletics.

When Reggie was born, his parents were concerned about Reggie walking. Sports were not even a thought. (AP/Wide World Photos)

3

Standing Tall

Reggie Miller's first steps came with steel braces on his legs and corrective shoes on his feet. At birth, Carrie and Saul Miller wondered if their son would ever walk at all, let alone participate in athletics.

A defect resulted in Reggie being born with his legs and hips contorted and twisted.

"My mother cried when I was born," Reggie said in his book *I Love Being the Enemy* (with Gene

Wojciechowski; New York: Simon & Schuster, 1995). "The doctors said I might not ever walk and (not to) think about playing sports."

Unable to take part in the fun and games, Reggie became a spectator. He would sit in his kitchen and watch his brothers and sisters and other children play.

When the family moved to Riverside, California, Saul built a basketball court in the backyard.

Reggie's sisters—Cheryl and Tammy—and his brothers—Saul Jr. and Darrell—were star athletes as kids. They were on their way to becoming playground legends in Riverside. Since Reggie couldn't participate, he made the best of the situation observing.

Cheryl showed outstanding skill at an early age, and she received a great deal of coaching from her father.

"I had to have braces and I had them up to the

age of 4 or 5," Reggie said in an interview with *NBA Inside Stuff Magazine* (June 21, 1995 issue).

"I remember I wasn't able to go outside and play with Cheryl or my brothers. But my parents kept me positive. I know doctors said that I would never be able to run and play, but my parents were very persistent in making sure I did the same things as the other kids. They weren't going to let it affect the rest of my life."

Remaining positive, Reggie, and his family, never gave up hope. They prayed for a miracle, and remarkably it happened. As Reggie's body grew, his hips and legs began to correct themselves.

Reggie hit a growth spurt and stood 5-foot, 9-inches as a high school freshman. Once he was able to stand on his own two feet, his sisters—especially Cheryl—gave him no special treatment on the court. Cheryl routinely dominated when the

Reggie's toughest competition growing up came from his sister Cheryl. (Brian Spurlock)

two played one-on-one.

But it wasn't just Reggie getting his shots thrown back. All the kids in the neighborhood endured a similar fate when they challenged Cheryl. It reached the point that Reggie capitalized on his sister's skills, setting up one-on-one matchups with strangers for small wagers.

Cheryl's immense talents, and shot-blocking abilities, caused Reggie to adjust how he played. Since going to the basket was futile—Cheryl swatted away all his layup attempts—Reggie worked on his outside shot.

Gradually, he inched backwards, developing a high-arching, rainbow shot. He also worked on getting the shot off quicker.

Armed with a quick release and rainbow arch, Reggie found a way to score over taller opponents. Reggie's range eventually outgrew the family court. He took his jumper more than 20 feet from the basket, which meant he was stepping off the cement and into his mother's azalea garden.

"Shooting over people, that's just part of playing with older people," Reggie told *NBA Inside Stuff Magazine*. "You had to develop a quick release, high-arching shot. I had to come up with every advantage I could."

His determination and expert marksmanship made Reggie a high school basketball star. But basketball wasn't his only passion. He had a keen eye for hitting in baseball. At one point, his father thought Reggie would follow his brother Darrell into a baseball career.

Darrell became a baseball star. He spent five seasons with the California Angels.

The Miller children refined their baseball skills by playing a game they dubbed "corkball." If they didn't have a baseball to work with, they improvised by wrapping up a wine cork with lots of tape.

A broom handle was used as a bat.

While Reggie shoots with his right hand in basketball, he batted lefthanded in baseball. He became an excellent hitter. But instead of following Darrell's footsteps, basketball became his primary sport.

"Reggie always found a way to get it done," Darrell told *NBA Inside Stuff Magazine*. "(In basketball) you would kick the ball to him and he would shoot this high, high-arching shot."

As a high school basketball player, Reggie lived in the shadow of his sister, Cheryl.

Cheryl was dominating at Riverside Polytechnic when Reggie was a skinny 5-foot, 9-inch, 140-pounder. He tried to beef up by drinking lots of milk and eating constantly.

Despite being born with a handicap, Reggie worked himself into being one of the quickest players on the court. He first started dunking the bas-

Reggie's sister, Cheryl, was a member of the women's basketball team that won the gold medal at the 1984 Summer Olympics in Los Angeles. (AP/Wide World Photos)

ketball as a sophomore. He would practice by shooting between 500 and 700 shots a day. He would work on every imaginable angle—inside and outside.

Saul Miller gave Reggie pointers on how to be a better player; proper technique on his release, and how to follow his shot.

Reggie kept getting better, and more determined to somehow beat Cheryl. Yet, no matter what Reggie could do, Cheryl could do it better.

It was, of course, a credit to Cheryl, who went on to an outstanding collegiate career at the University of Southern California. Cheryl became a four-time All-American (1983-1986), and a three-time Naismith College Player of the Year. USC won two national championships in her tenure. She was named the 1980s Player of the Decade by the United States Basketball Writers Association. USC retired her uniform number. And she is a member of the Naismith Memorial Basketball Hall of Fame. Cheryl remains active in basketball as the coach of the Phoenix franchise in the WNBA. When not coaching, she serves as a basketball analyst.

In some circles, Cheryl Miller is still regarded as the best female basketball player ever.

In high school, Reggie had to live with the reputation of being "Cheryl's brother." Even at home, the Miller family had to split loyalties on nights Reggie and Cheryl played.

Reggie's father actively supported Cheryl, serving as an unofficial assistant coach for the girl's team. If there was a conflict in the schedule, Saul would attend his daughter's game. Meanwhile, Reggie's mom watched her son.

As fate would have it, history was made on a night both Reggie and Cheryl played.

With mom cheering him on, Reggie had a memorable 39-point performance. It was a breakout game, and confidence boost, for Reggie, who had struggled to crack the starting lineup.

An elated Reggie couldn't wait to alert the rest of his family. He and his mom arrived home to deliver the great news to Saul and Cheryl.

Reggie's joy was only outdone by Cheryl, who on the same night tossed in a state-record 105 points. Once again, his sister had shown him up. But Reggie never resented her for it. Reggie says Cheryl's achievement remains one of the greatest days of his life.

"I think he had to handle a lot of different things at a very early age," Cheryl told NBA Inside Stuff Magazine. "That helped him and I think it will continue to help him. I think the big thing he has learned is there is no obstacle too big to overcome."

The child who was once told he would never walk was about to take a big step to the college level.

Reggie slowly built his own reputation in high school and earned a scholarship at UCLA. (photo courtesy UCLA)

Becoming a Bruin

Cheryl may have been a four-time *Parade Magazine* high school All-American, but she wasn't the only Miller making headlines in high school.

Gradually, Reggie emerged from his sister's shadow. His big break as a prepster came when a teammate inadvertently brought the wrong color jersey to a road game, leaving Riverside Poly down a player. The coach called on Reggie to start. As a replacement, the untested sophomore pumped in

35 points.

Reggie capitalized on the opportunity, and he became a regular in the starting lineup. Showing his first-game heroics was not a fluke, Reggie tossed in 45 points in the very next game.

At last, all the hours playing in his backyard, losing to his sister, were paying off.

Reggie's body kept growing, and so did the accuracy of his long-range jumper. A constant in his upbringing was a supportive family. His father worked with him on the finer points of the game.

Reggie was well on his way to a stellar basketball career. But was basketball his best sport?

As skilled as he was shooting a ball, he was just as good hitting a baseball. His brother, Darrell, was already a standout on the diamond.

Reggie could have had a promising baseball career, but something about the sport turned him off.

"I was standing in the outfield one day and it was cold," Reggie is quoted saying in the book *I Love Being the Enemy.* "The wind was whistling, and nobody was hitting the ball to me. That's when I decided I needed something nonstop. I needed that excitement, that adrenaline to get me going."

By the time Reggie was a senior, he achieved the status as the best male basketball player in California. He also helped lead Riverside Polytechnic High School to a California divisional championship.

Reggie was flooded with scholarship offers from interested colleges. Cheryl, a year older than Reggie, was already at the University of Southern California.

In order for Reggie to create his own identity, he felt going to another school was in his best interest. So storied UCLA, the most decorated col-

Reggie was the first sophomore to lead UCLA in scoring since Bill Walton. (photo courtesy UCLA)

lege basketball program ever, became his choice.

Reggie aspired to add his name to a long list of Bruins legends including, Lew Alcindor (Kareem Abdul-Jabbar), Bill Walton, Don MacLean, Jamaal Wilkes, Michael Warren, Kiki Vandeweghe, Sidney Wicks, Henry Bibby, Lucius Allen and Lynn Shackleford.

In Reggie's sophomore season, Walt Hazzard replaced Larry Farmer as UCLA's head coach. Reggie's career began to take off.

Hazzard encouraged Reggie to shoot those long-range "rainbow" jumpers. Reggie became the workhorse on the team, missing just 27 of the team's 715 minutes over their final 17 games.

The Bruins advanced to the National Invitation Tournament in that 1984-85 season. Miller became the school's first sophomore to lead UCLA in scoring since Bill Walton.

UCLA advanced to the tournament's semifinals at Madison Square Garden, the site where the Bruins suffered an embarrassing 88-69 loss during the regular season to St. John's.

The Bruins, however, had made great progress down the stretch. This time, they traveled to New York primed to win a championship.

In the semifinals, the Bruins knocked off Louisville, 75-66. That set up a meeting in the NIT championship game against Bob Knight and the Indiana Hoosiers.

Indiana that year was led by guard Steve Alford.

Like Miller, Alford was a sophomore guard with the reputation as a long-range sharp shooter. The two dueled head-to-head. In the early stages, Alford got the better of the action. But a jump shot by Reggie Miller tied the game at halftime.

In the end, Reggie got hot, and UCLA held on

for a 65-62 victory. Reggie was named the tournament MVP in a close vote over Alford.

For Reggie, it was a shining moment in a nationally televised game. It also quieted his critics.

"A magazine article said Reggie couldn't beat his sister one-on-one," Coach Hazzard said. "I wish the writer would put some salt and pepper on it and eat that article."

It was sweet redemption for Reggie.

"This is really sweet," he told reporters after the game. "We and the coach took a lot of verbal abuse."

Reggie wasn't just Cheryl's younger brother any longer. He was a bonafide big-time college basketball player.

As a junior and senior, he established himself as a pure scorer. His scoring average as a junior was 26 points per game, fourth highest in the country.

*Reggie stepped completely out of Cheryl's shadow when
he was named MVP of the NIT tournament in 1985.
(photo courtesy UCLA)*

When Reggie was a senior, college basketball added a 3-point shot rule, awarding an extra point for shots made beyond a 19-feet, 9-inch circle.

The rule was ideal for Reggie, who often connected from distances much farther than 19-9.

Reggie completed his college career ranking third all-time in scoring in UCLA history with 2,095 points. In his final season in Westwood, Reggie hit 59 percent of his final 200 shots from the field, including 57.6 percent from 3-point range (34 of 59) over the last 14 games of the year.

Reggie Miller was clearly a shooting star, with his stock rising in the 1987 NBA draft.

Reggie was not a popular choice when the Pacers chose him in the 1987 NBA draft. (AP/Wide World Photos)

CHAPTER FIVE

Indiana Wants Him

Holding the 11th overall pick in the 1987 draft, the Indiana Pacers' needs were clear. They wanted a sharp-shooter, a natural scorer with excellent outside range. In basketball-crazy Indiana, the local residents believed the Pacers didn't need to go outside the state to find their man.

By all accounts, Steve Alford should have been the pick. Alford, after all, was the pride of Indiana, a homegrown hero who helped the Indiana Hoosiers win the national championship. To the natives, going with Alford was a no-brainer. Alford could shoot. He could help the Pacers sell tickets. He would bring a Midwestern work ethic.

Steve Alford, in essence, represented all the virtues Indiana residents aspired in their athletes.

But there is an old saying: "What's popular isn't always right, and what's right isn't always popular."

When it came decision time, the Pacers went in another direction. They selected a slender 6-7, 165-pound shooter from UCLA named Reggie Miller.

Initially, the local fans were upset. But ultimately, the Pacers made the correct choice.

Alford never amounted to much in a short career that started in Dallas. Since hanging it up as a player, Alford has become a successful college head coach and is now at the University of Iowa.

Reggie Miller, meanwhile, has become the all-time scoring leader for the Pacers. Even as a rookie, it didn't take him long to become a crowd favorite.

But success didn't come immediately. Like everyone, he went through some growing pains performing at the highest level of the sport. It reflected in his scoring average, a career-low 10 points a game.

What fans saw in the rookie from UCLA was that famous shooting touch. Reggie was remarkably accurate, hitting nearly 49 percent of his shots from the field. From the foul line, always a strength, he was an excellent 80 percent.

Reggie did leave a mark in his first year, setting a rookie record for most total 3-point baskets, 61. That number has since been broken, but at the time, Reggie surpassed the previously high total once held by the great Larry Bird, who eventually would become Reggie's coach.

As a rookie, Reggie broke a record held by his future coach, Larry Bird. (AP/Wide World Photos)

Reggie's production greatly picked up in his second season. In a campaign where he averaged 16 points per game, he was named to the 1990 Eastern Conference All-Star team, the first Pacer to achieve All-Star status since 1977.

From a statistical standpoint, Reggie's best season was his third. Entrenching himself as an elite talent, his scoring average climbed to 24.6 points per game. The ever-accurate Reggie shot an eye-popping .514 percent, an outstanding figure considering his reputation as a bomber.

At last, Reggie—the kid who was once kidded about failing to beat his sister—had established himself as a star among NBA stars.

By 1990, Reggie had replaced Chuck Person as the Pacers' number one scoring option. Officially, he was the team's "go-to-guy." He has lived up to the expectations, leading the Pacers in scoring average every year in the 1990s.

In fact, Reggie Miller is the only player in the NBA to lead his team in scoring average every season in the decade. Not even the fabulous Michael Jordan accomplished this feat. M.J. may have equaled the feat, but he took a break from basketball to take a shot at a pro baseball career.

From 1990-94, Reggie averaged more than 20 points a season. The single-game highlight of his career came in 1992 when he turned in a career-high 57 points (still a franchise NBA record) at Charlotte. Not only could Reggie score from anywhere on the floor, he hardly missed. For three straight seasons in the early 1990s, he shot better than 50 percent from the floor.

Combine his long-range touch and a career 88 percent free throw average, and Reggie Miller is one of the top scoring threats in all of basketball.

In addition to being recognized as one of the best players in the league, his name has become known world-wide, as well.

Disappointed about failing to make "Dream Team One" at the 1992 Olympics in Barcelona, Spain, Reggie got another chance at international stardom two years later.

Reggie was a member of "Dream Team Two" at the World Basketball Championships in Toronto, Canada. A roster spot opened with the retirement of Isiah Thomas, and Reggie Miller capitalized.

The NBA was going through a transition period then. Leading up to the 1994 World Basketball Championships, the league witnessed the retirements of Larry Bird, Magic Johnson, Isiah Thomas and Michael Jordan (to baseball).

Dream Team II represented a passing of the torch to a new set of rising stars. Shaquille O'Neal, Alonzo Mourning, Larry Johnson and Shawn Kemp

Reggie, third from the right, listens to the national anthem with the members of Dream Team II after winning the gold medal in the 1996 Summer Olympics in Atlanta. (AP/Wide World Photos)

shared the spotlight with Reggie.

Like the first group of Dream Teamers, the 1994 U.S. team breezed through the competition, only rarely being tested. They were challenged briefly in their opening game, but still prevailed rather easily, 115-100 over Spain.

From that point, the U.S. stars cruised through its next seven games. Reggie was a tri-captain who demonstrated the kind of leadership on the All-Star team that the Indiana Pacers had come to expect.

On a star-studded squad, Reggie was second on his team in scoring with a 17 points per game average. His 30 3-point baskets were the most in the entire tournament. His highest scoring output was 31 points against Australia. In a rout over Puerto Rico, he connected on eight of 11 3-point baskets.

By the time gold medals were draped around the United States' players necks, the name Reggie Miller was known world wide.

Beating the Knicks is even sweeter for Reggie because of his history with Knicks super-fan, Spike Lee. (AP/Wide World Photos)

6

Reggie vs. Spike

The NBA has always had its share of outstanding individual rivalries. Wilt Chamberlain vs. Bill Russell, Jerry West vs. Oscar Robertson, and Larry Bird vs. Magic Johnson are some of the all-time great matchups.

Reggie Miller's No. 1 nemesis, strangely, is not another player—although he and Michael Jordan had their share of heated moments.

History will link Reggie with super-fan and filmmaker Spike Lee. Lee is a fixture sitting courtside at Madison Square Garden, where he feverishly cheers on his beloved New York Knicks. Often clad in a Knicks jersey, Spike likes to mix it up with opposing players, frequently exchanges words and taunts during games.

The heat of battle in Game 5 of the 1994 play-offs between the Pacers and Knicks ignited the first of several Reggie Miller/Spike Lee feuds.

New York headed into the fourth quarter with a lead, but in the final 12 minutes Reggie made history and as well as a courtside enemy.

Stunning the New York crowd, Reggie rallied the Pacers with 25 points in the quarter, including a playoff record five 3-point baskets in the period. The Pacers' top scorer rubbed it in on Lee, staring down the filmmaker after every made basket.

Indiana went on to win Game 5 in memorable fashion, 93-86, on a night Reggie Miller didn't win over any friends in New York.

The Knicks, however, eventually eliminated the Pacers from the 1994 playoffs, but the seed was planted for more Reggie/Spike encounters the following season.

Tired of being bullied by the overly-aggressive Knicks, the Pacers finally tasted revenge in the 1995 playoffs, taking the series in seven action-packed games.

Reggie Miller's defining moments, however, came in the closing seconds of Game One. At Madison Square Garden, the Knicks enjoyed a six-point lead with 16.4 seconds remaining before Reggie pulled off the unthinkable.

In a span of 8.9 seconds, Reggie scored eight points, lifting the Pacers to an unlikely 107-105 victory.

Reggie's rally started with a 3-point basket that

As good as he is, Reggie is even better at Madison Square Garden.
(AP/Wide World Photos)

closed the game to 105-102. On the ensuing inbounds pass, Anthony Mason of the Knicks tried to get the ball to teammate Greg Anthony. Guard Byron Scott of the Pacers was fronting Greg Anthony and Reggie sandwiched Anthony from behind.

Greg Anthony ended up falling, and Anthony Mason's pass went straight to Reggie, who took a few steps back beyond the 3-point line and then delivered the game-tying shot with 13.3 seconds to go.

A few seconds later, Reggie delivered the crushing blow to the Knicks, two decisive free throws. Reggie finished with 31 points—matching his jersey number. The Knicks walked off the court in disbelief.

"In my wildest imagination, I never thought we could win this game in regulation," then Pacers coach Larry Brown told reporters.

Reggie reveled in the victory like never before. He taunted the Madison Square Garden crowd, Spike Lee, and eventually the Knicks players.

"In the game, (Reggie) loses his head so much, he doesn't realize his actions," Spike Lee told the New York media. "He lost his mind."

Game One of the 1995 playoffs best demonstrated how Reggie Miller plays up being the unpopular opponent. He put the pressure of the series on his boney shoulders, but never backed down.

Trash talking has long been part of professional sports. And few in the NBA could talk and deliver as well as Reggie.

Reggie was heard calling the Knicks "chokers" while running off the court.

After the game, Reggie spoke his mind to *New York Post* columnist Peter Vecsey, who also is an analyst for NBC.

Vecsey's column ran in the Post on May 9, 1995, and it became the talk of the series.

"Did I lose control of my emotions?" Reggie asked Vecsey. "Put yourself in my shoes. It was like winning the lottery. What are the Knicks going to do now, make me eat my words? We're not intimidated. Those days are over."

Reggie felt compelled to speak his mind because he claimed the Knicks showed an absolute lack of respect for the Pacers.

"I wouldn't have said a word if they gave me respect," Reggie told Vecsey. "But the Knicks are the biggest prima donnas I know. They think they are God's gift to basketball. They might respect the Bulls and the Magic, but they definitely don't respect us."

The Vecsey column added that prior to Game One, word leaked out of the Knicks locker room that New York would try to rough up Indiana's 7-4

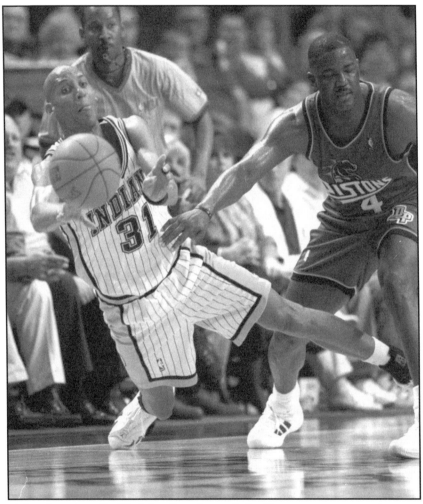

After beating the Knicks, Reggia and the Pacers were not going to be intimidated by anyone. (AP/Wide World Photos)

center Rik Smits. Upon hearing those remarks, the Pacers assembled for a players-only team meeting. They decided to meet force with force. In the course of the game, there was an exchange of words from Pacers forward Antonio Davis and Knicks guard Derek Harper. A confrontation also took place between Knicks forward Charles Oakley and the Pacers bench.

For a few seasons, tensions had run high when the Knicks and Pacers played. Reggie uncorked his emotions after a thrilling win.

Peter Vecsey told Reggie he went over the line with the comment that the Knicks were chokers. And Vecsey said Reggie's comments may have diminished his outstanding achievement.

"There is no way I tainted what I did," Reggie said in the Post column. "Why, just because I said what other people were thinking. Just because I said what everyone was saying in the stands? Just because I said what every writer probably wrote?

Byron Scott told *The Indianapolis Star*: "That's (Reggie) and it gets him involved. I don't think he needs to do it for us, but for him, he needs to do it. He needs to think that everything is on his shoulders, and I think it makes him play better."

Pacers teammate Vern Fleming said to *The Indianapolis Star*: "That's how he gets himself pumped up for games. If you were a spectator, and you watched the game, you would have said the same thing he did about Game One. They choked. That's Reg."

Despite the controversy, Reggie never backed down from his statements. "If it came out of my mouth, I've never regretted saying anything," he told reporters after the Peter Vecsey column ran.

Ironically, Reggie's outburst on the court and

his outrageous comments afterward made him a national celebrity.

"A couple of more exciting moments like yesterday's and (Reggie) will take off," David Burns, president of the Burns Celebrity Sports Service in Chicago, said to the *New York Times* in a May 9, 1995 article. "He is anything but local now."

Brandon Steiner, president of Steiner Sports Marketing said in the same *Times* article: "(Reggie) is a real camera-ready guy. Before Jordan came back (from baseball retirement), a lot of eyes were on guys like Reggie, Chris Webber and Anfernee Hardaway."

Shortly after the 1995 playoffs, Reggie appeared in advertisements with his sister Cheryl. And he landed a cameo appearance in the Billy Crystal movie "Forget Paris."

"It doesn't matter what I say or don't say," Reggie told Peter Vecsey. "People are still going to

Reggie's finger-roll is another of his signature shots. (AP/Wide World Photos)

perceive me in the same way."

Actually, after the Pacers eliminated the Knicks in seven games, people learned more about what makes Reggie Miller. Private off the court, he reveals only glimpses of himself on the court.

On the court, he thrives on playing the role of the enemy. But like all performers, that image is largely an act.

While he enjoys playing the bad guy, Reggie does a lot of charity work. (AP/Wide World Photos)

CHAPTER SEVEN

The Enemy Has a Heart

Beneath the enemy image Reggie likes to project on the court is a generous and intelligent person. A man who has repeatedly bounced back from adversity; constantly turning negatives into positives.

He especially has a soft spot for children, frequently making surprise visits to elementary schools in the Indianapolis area. He contributes to several children's charities, including Riley Hospital for Children in Indianapolis. He has been honored by the Make-A-Wish Foundation.

He is the national spokesperson for the Reading is Fundamental Program.

In 1996, Reggie encountered more personal tragedy when his multi-million dream home in Indianapolis was set on fire by someone. The house burned to the ground. Police have not yet found the person responsible for the incident.

Once again, Reggie is making the best of an awful situation. The Reggie Miller Foundation has been established to assist fire victims.

Prior to the 1999 playoffs, Reggie raised awareness for his foundation at a charity bowling event in Noblesville, Indiana, a small community about 30 miles north of Indianapolis. Reggie and his actress/model wife Marita Stavrou hosted the event by inviting many celebrities, including Indianapolis Colts quarterback Peyton Manning and the pop-music sensations, 'N Sync.

"Marita and I were somewhat hesitant about putting something of this magnitude on." Reggie told the large gathering in the bowling alley. "After the loss of our home to arson (1996), we were wondering if something good could come from something so bad. And, seeing all the screaming fans, it's clear that it can. So give yourselves a big round of applause.

"It's really to help young kids who were burned in fires and their families—skin graphs, send them to camp. A lot of kids who are burnt don't have the opportunity to go to camp. All of the proceeds are going to help kids and their families deal with the emotional, physical and psychological scars left by the fires. ... Two years ago, my wife and myself

**In any kind of competition, Reggie hates to lose.
(AP/Wide World Photos)**

lost our home to fire. We had the resources to rebuild, but there's a lot of kids and a lot of families who don't have that opportunity. This is a way to give back to them.

"Everyone believes they can bowl. Everyone talks a good game in bowling. What better way to put their mouths and money on the line than to have a bowling tournament? To the corporate sponsors who opened their hearts and their wallets and gave their time—a lot of you guys, I'm close personal friends with. And I really do appreciate you guys. Because it's not about the Pacers or myself. It's about the kids and the families who are gonna benefit from this. This money is gonna help these children out, as well as their families. So thank you so much to everyone."

Even in a fun-filled event, Reggie Miller's competitive juices were flowing, especially against his teammate and buddy, Mark Jackson.

"I'm gonna tell you right now, Mark has been practicing for this for two months," Reggie said in a good-natured ribbing with Jackson. "He is gonna try to tell me that he hasn't been working on his bowling. But he is a part-time bowler."

Mark Jackson shot back: "Reggie Miller talked so much trash on the way to the bowling alley that somewhere on the way, he must have left his game prior to entering the building."

Trash-talking aside, Mark Jackson told the people in attendance: "This is what it's all about—taking the time to give back. I take my hat off to Reggie Miller for giving back. And all the guys who came here—football players, entertainers, businessmen—they're coming out here and giving of themselves to a very worthy cause. It's an honor to be part of it."

When it came time to knocking down pins, Reggie gave the rest of the competitors a warning.

"There's gonna be a lot of gutter balls on those other teams," Reggie said. "I tell the competition that I am, and truthfully, I'm probably the best non-professional bowler around here."

Reggie Miller has never doubted his ability. He's immensely confident, and yet, very loyal.

Through the years, he has given his all to the Indiana Pacers. There was a time he probably could have left the team, opting for greener pastures in a bigger market, like New York or Los Angeles.

Speculation in 1996 had Reggie moving on when his contract expired. As a free agent, he could have moved on. The Knicks, in search of a scorer, would have made a natural fit. Or Reggie could have gone home, back to Los Angeles and signed on with the Lakers. In a bigger city, Reggie could have attracted more fame.

The situation with Pacers that season was also in decline. The team struggled on the court, falling from the ranks of the league's elite. Coach Larry Brown was fired after four seasons.

It was an ideal time to leave but the Pacers stepped up with an attractive offer of nearly $36 million over four seasons. So instead of restarting his career elsewhere, Reggie Miller accepted Indiana's deal.

In an age where so many athletes jump from team-to-team, Reggie wants stability.

"A lot of kids have grown up watching Reggie Miller and identify with me," Reggie was quoted in the *1997-1998 Official Indiana Pacers Team Yearbook* (New York: Finlay Sports, 1998). "To me, one of the things that has hurt sports the most is the kids seeing these guys moving around. Coming in and playing in one place your whole career stands for something.

Reggie has played his entire NBA career with the Indiana Pacers.
(AP/Wide World Photos)

Reggie Miller Quick Facts

Full Name: Reginald Wayne Miller

Team: Indiana Pacers

Position: Guard

Jersey Number: 31

Height/Weight: 6' 7"/ 185 lbs.

Years in League: 13

Drafted: 11th overall in 1987

College: UCLA

Birthdate: August 24, 1965

Hometown: Riverside, California

1999 Highlight: Reggie led the Pacers in scoring for the 10th straight year, averaging 18.4 points per game.

Statistical Spotlight: Reggie is the Pacers' all-time leading scorer, with 18,322 career points going into the 1999-2000 season. His 1,072 three-point baskets are the most in NBA history.

Little Known Fact: Reggie has appeared in the feature films *Forget Paris* and *Gang Related*. He has also made numerous television appearances.

Reggie Miller's NBA Statistics

Career Totals

Year	Games	FG/FGA	FT/FTA	3P/3PA	Ast	Pts
1987-88	82	306/627	149/186	61/172	132	822
1988-89	74	398/831	287/340	98/244	227	1,181
1989-90	82	661/1,287	544/627	150/362	311	2,016
1990-91	82	596/1,164	551/600	112/322	331	1,855
1991-92	82	562/1,121	442/515	129/341	314	1,695
1992-93	82	571/1,193	427/485	167/419	262	1,736
1993-94	79	524/1,042	403/444	123/292	248	1,574
1994-95	81	505/1,092	383/427	195/470	242	1,588
1995-96	76	504/1,066	430/498	168/410	253	1,606
1996-97	81	552/1,244	418/475	229/536	273	1,751
1997-98	81	516/1,081	382/440	164/382	171	1,578
1998-99	50	294/671	226/247	106/275	112	920
Totals	932	5,989/12,419	4,642/5284	1,702/4,225	2,876	18,322

Career Averages

Year	Games	FG%	FT%	3P%	APG	PPG
1987-88	82	.488	.801	.355	1.6	10.0
1988-89	74	.479	.844	.402	3.1	16.0
1989-90	82	.514	.868	.414	3.8	24.6
1990-91	82	.512	.918	.348	4.0	22.6
1991-92	82	.501	.858	.378	3.8	20.7
1992-93	82	.479	.880	.399	3.2	21.2
1993-94	79	.503	.908	.421	3.1	19.9
1994-95	81	.462	.897	.415	3.0	19.6
1995-96	76	.473	.863	.410	3.3	21.1
1996-97	81	.444	.880	.427	3.4	21.6
1997-98	81	.477	.868	.429	2.1	19.5
1998-99	50	.438	.915	.385	2.2	18.4
Totals	**77.7**	**.482**	**.879**	**.403**	**3.1**	**19.7**

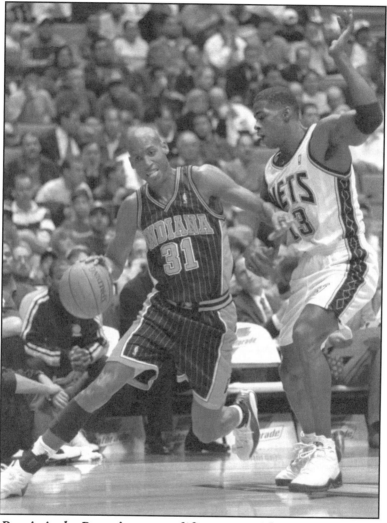

Reggie is the Pacers' most prolific scorer with 18,322 points. (AP/Wide World Photos)

1999 Free Throw Percentage Leaders

1.	**Reggie Miller, Indiana**	**.915**
2.	Chauncey Billups, Denver	.913
3.	Darrell Armstrong, Orlando	.904
4.	Ray Allen, Milwaukee	.903
5.	Hersey Hawkins, Seattle	.902
6.	Jeff Hornacek, Utah	.893
7.	Glenn Robinson, Milwaukee	.870
8.	Chris Mullin, Indiana	.870
9.	Mario Elie, San Antonio	.866
10.	Eric Piatkowski, L.A. Clippers	.863

1999 Three-Point Shots Made Leaders

1.	Dee Brown, Toronto	135
2.	Tim Hardaway, Miama	112
3.	**Reggie Miller, Indiana**	**106**
4.	Jason Williams, Sacramento	100
5.	Nick Anderson, Orlando	96
6.	Dale Ellis, Seattle	94
7.	Joe Dumars, Detroit	89
8.	Sam Mack, Houston	87
9.	Chauncey Billups, Denver	85
10.	Paul Pierce, Boston	84

Career Three-Point Shots Made Leaders (Through the 1998-99 Season)

1.	**Reggie Miller**	**1,702**
2.	Dale Ellis	1,682
3.	Glen Rice	1,269
4.	Chuck Person	1,196
5.	Mitch Richmond	1,170
6.	Vernon Maxwell	1,155
7.	Hersey Hawkins	1,154
8.	Dennis Scott	1,143
9.	Tim Hardaway	1,125
10.	Dan Majerle	1,114

Baseball Superstar Series Titles

Collect Them All!

___ Mark McGwire: Mac Attack!

___ #1 *Derek Jeter: The Yankee Kid*

___ #2 *Ken Griffey Jr.: The Home Run Kid*

___ #3 *Randy Johnson: Arizona Heat!*

___ #4 *Sammy Sosa: Slammin' Sammy*

___ #5 *Bernie Williams: Quiet Superstar*

___ #6 *Omar Vizquel: The Man with the Golden Glove*

___ #7 *Mo Vaughn: Angel on a Mission*

___ #8 *Pedro Martinez: Throwing Strikes*

___ #9 *Juan Gonzalez: Juan Gone!*

___ #10 *Tony Gwynn: Mr. Padre*

___ #11 *Kevin Brown: Kevin with a "K"*

___ #12 *Mike Piazza: Mike and the Mets*

___ #13 *Larry Walker: Canadian Rocky*

___ #14 *Nomar Garciaparra: High 5!*

___ #15 *Sandy and Roberto Alomar: Baseball Brothers*

___ #16 *Mark Grace: Winning with Grace*

___ #17 *Curt Schilling: Phillie Phire!*

___ #18 *Alex Rodriguez: A+ Shortstop*

___ #19 *Roger Clemens: Rocket!*

Only $4.95 per book!

Call Toll Free: 1-877-424-BOOK (2665) or visit us at www.sportspublishinginc.com

Football Superstar Series Titles
Collect Them All!

Only $4.95 per book!

**Call Toll Free: 1-877-424-BOOK (2665) or
visit us at www.sportspublishinginc.com**

Basketball Superstar Series Titles
Collect Them All!

____ #1 *Kobe Bryant: The Hollywood Kid*

____ #2 *Keith Van Horn: Nothing But Net*

____ #3 *Antoine Walker: Kentucky Celtic*

____ #4 *Kevin Garnett: Scratching the Surface*

____ #5 *Tim Duncan: Slam Duncan*

____ #6 *Reggie Miller: From Downtown*

____ #7 *Jason Kidd: Rising Sun*

____ #8 *Vince Carter: Air Canada*

Only $4.95 per book!

NASCAR Superstar Series Titles

Hockey Superstar Series Titles

Only $4.95 per book!

Collect Them All!

Call Toll Free: 1-877-424-BOOK (2665) or visit us at www.sportspublishinginc.com